Discovering Science

WEATHER

Rebecca Hunter

RAINTREE
STECK-VAUGHN
PUBLISHERS

A Harcourt Company

Austin   New York
www.steck-vaughn.com

Published by Raintree Steck-Vaughn Publishers, an imprint of Steck-Vaughn Company

Acknowledgments
Project Editors: Rebecca Hunter, Pam Wells
Art Director: Max Brinkmann
Illustrated by Pamela Goodchild, Stefan Chabluk, and Keith Williams
Designed by Ian Winton

Planned and produced by Discovery Books

Library of Congress Cataloging-in-Publication Data
Hunter, Rebecca (Rebecca K. de C.)
Weather / Rebecca Hunter.
p. cm. — (Discovering science)
Includes index.
ISBN 0-7398-3245-X
1. Weather—Juvenile literature. [.Weather.] I. Title.

QC981.3 .H87 2001
551.6—dc21
00-042451
CIP AC

1 2 3 4 5 6 7 8 9 0 BNG 05 04 03 02 01
Printed and bound in the United States of America.

Note to the reader: You will find difficult words in the glossary on page 30.

CONTENTS

What's the Weather?

Take a look outside. What's the weather like? Is it sunny or is it raining? Perhaps there is snow on the ground. Whatever the weather is like today, you can be sure of one thing. It will be different tomorrow. It may be slightly cooler or slightly warmer. It might be more cloudy, or rainy. The weather will hardly ever be exactly the same.

How the Weather Affects Us

Many of the things we do, what we wear, and what we eat are affected by the weather. When it is cold, we stay indoors or dress up warmly if we have to go outside. We eat more hot meals and drink hot things to warm us up.

In the summer when the days are long and sunny, we might head for the beach or pool. We wear fewer clothes, and we like to eat ice cream and drink cold beverages.

On a wet day we wear raincoats and carry an umbrella. Umbrellas are not much good on windy days, but kites are. We can fly them!

WHAT IS WEATHER?

Weather is decided by things such as wind, rain, clouds, and sunshine.

WORLD WEATHER

The weather is different all over the world. It may be different from state to state and even from city to city. In many parts of the world, the weather changes with the seasons. Summers usually bring hotter weather with brief showers or heavy thunderstorms. But winters are colder and may even be snowy.

A rainbow appears during showers in Hawaii.

PREDICTING THE WEATHER

It would be nice always to know what the weather will be like tomorrow. By learning what causes the weather and being able to understand some of its signs, we can try to predict, or foretell, what is going to happen.

◄ It can be fun walking in the rain – if you are dressed for it!

THE ATMOSPHERE

Weather is caused by changes in the atmosphere.

The atmosphere is the name we give to the layer of gases around Earth. The atmosphere is about 620 miles (1,000 km) thick.

Nearly all clouds form in the bottom 6-7 miles (10-12 km) of the atmosphere, and this is where most of the weather happens.

HEATING THE EARTH

Earth is heated by the Sun. Different parts of Earth receive different amounts of heat. Places along the equator are the hottest places on Earth because the Sun heats this area from directly overhead. The North and South poles are the coldest places because Earth's surface is curved, so the Sun's rays are spread out over a wider area.

THERMOMETERS

We can tell how hot or cold a place is by measuring the temperature of the air with a thermometer. A thermometer is a tube that contains a liquid. This liquid rises up the tube as it is heated and falls as it cools. A scale is printed next to it. The scale is like the scale on a ruler. But, instead of measuring in inches or centimeters, a thermometer measures in degrees Celsius (°C) or Fahrenheit (°F).

PROJECT

What is the temperature where you live?

You will need

A garden thermometer
A note pad

1. Hang the thermometer in an open space in your backyard, but make sure it is in the shade. The side of your garage or the trunk of a tree would be a good place.

2. Look at the level of liquid in the thermometer, and write the temperature you see in the notepad.

3. Measure the temperature at the same time every day. The day will probably be warmest at around 2:00PM. Try to take the temperature as close to this time as possible – maybe when you come home from school.

4. Write your results in a chart.

5. Do this at different times of the year. Then you will be able to see the change in temperature from season to season.

WIND

Air that moves across Earth's surface is called wind. But what makes the air move?

When air is heated, it rises. You can see this happening when a hot-air balloon takes off. Gas burners heat the air inside the balloon. When the air is hot enough, the whole balloon is lifted off the ground into the sky.

MOVING AIR

A similar thing happens when the Sun heats the land. The warm land heats the air above it, and the warmed air starts to rise. In other parts of the atmosphere, air is cooling down. Cool air sinks down. The cold air moves in to take the place of the warm air rising in other places. This movement of air across the land is what we call a wind.

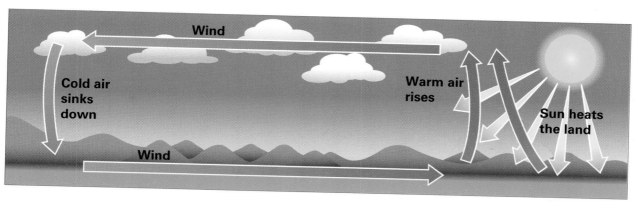

Wind

Cold air sinks down

Warm air rises

Sun heats the land

Wind

WORLD WINDS

This map shows some of the winds that blow across Earth. These global winds are called trade winds because sailing ships once counted on them to carry goods around the world.

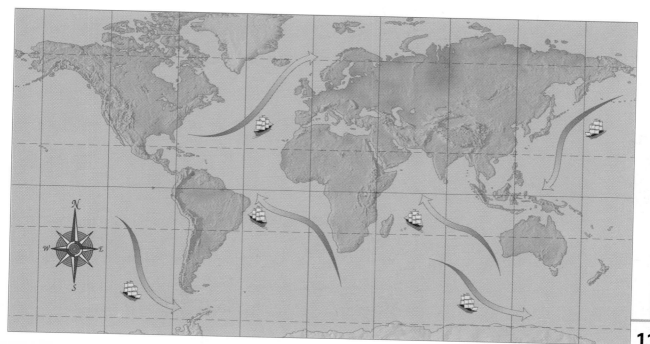

MEASURING THE WIND

We can record the wind in two ways. We can look at its direction and measure its speed.

WIND DIRECTION

We always record the direction a wind is coming from. A westerly wind is coming from the west, an easterly wind from the east, and so on. We record wind direction using a weather vane. You might have seen a weather vane on top of a tall building such as a church tower.

WIND SPEED

In 1805, Admiral Sir Francis Beaufort worked out a scale for measuring wind speed. This scale is called the Beaufort Scale and is still used today. It measures wind speed from air that is barely moving (Force 1) through to a full-scale hurricane (Force 12). Wind speed is measured with a device called an anemometer.

BEAUFORT SCALE

1. Smoke drifts gently.

2. Leaves rustle.

3. Leaves and twigs on trees move.

4. Flags flutter.

5. Small branches move.

6. Large branches move.

PROJECT

Make a weather vane.

You will need
A drinking straw
A pin
A bead
A cork
A wooden garden stake
Some colored cardboard
Scissors
Clear tape

1. Make a short cut lengthways in each end of the straw.

2. Cut a pointed fish head and tail (or any other animal) and push into the ends of the straw.

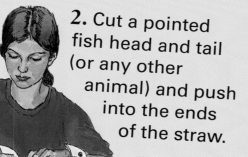

3. Fix the cork with clear tape to the garden stake.

4. Push the pin through the balance point of the straw, then through the bead and into the cork.

5. Push the stake into the ground in an open space.

6. Ask an adult to show you where north is, and mark with an N on the cork. Mark the positions of south, west, and east in the same way.

7. Whole trees sway.

8. Limbs break off trees.

9. Tiles blow off roofs.

10. Trees blown down.

11. Serious damage to property.

12. Hurricane – wind speed over 75 mph.

CLOUDS

Clouds are a good way to predict the kind of weather to expect in the next few hours or days. A sky full of dark, thick clouds almost certainly means rain. Fluffy, white clouds that form on sunny days mean the weather will probably stay warm and dry.

WHAT ARE CLOUDS MADE OF?

This may sound strange, but clouds are made of water. Water can exist in three forms. We usually see it as a liquid in lakes and rivers or coming out of a faucet. If we freeze it, it becomes a solid called ice. The third form of water is a gas called water vapor.

EVAPORATION AND CONDENSATION

Water vapor cannot be seen, but the air is always full of it. On a sunny day, a puddle of water will quickly dry up. The water has not really disappeared, it has turned into water vapor in the air. When a liquid turns into a gas, it is called evaporation.

When water vapor cools down, it will turn back into tiny drops of liquid water. Water vapor turning into water again is called condensation. If you breathe onto a cold window, the water vapor in your breath condenses into tiny droplets of water on the window pane.

Water vapor from a kettle condenses on a cold window.

Water vapor evaporates from rivers, lakes, and oceans all the time. Clouds form when warm air carrying this water vapor rises. Air rises when it is warmed by the land, or when the wind pushes it up and over hills.

As the air rises, it cools, and the water vapor condenses into tiny water droplets. These tiny droplets join together to make clouds. Each cloud is made of millions of tiny droplets of water.

Types of Clouds

There are three main types of clouds:

Stratus clouds form as sheets of low gray clouds, that often cover the whole sky. They usually mean light rain or drizzle.

Cumulus clouds mean fine weather. They look like giant puffs of cotton and are formed on sunny days.

These are typical cumulus clouds.

Cirrus clouds are thin, wispy clouds that are very high up in the sky. At this level it is so cold that the clouds are not made of water droplets but tiny ice crystals. They often appear with wind and mean the weather is going to change.

These wispy clouds are cirrus clouds.

How Cloudy Is It?

The amount of cloud cover is measured by working out how much of the sky is actually covered by clouds. This can be shown by drawing a circle and partly shading it in.

No clouds in sky.

A few clouds present.

Half the sky is covered with clouds.

Clouds cover most of the sky.

The sky is completely filled with cloud cover.

This method makes it easy to write down how much cloud cover is present. Look outside now. How much cloud cover is there? What symbol would you draw?

17

RAIN, SNOW, AND HAIL

THE WATER CYCLE

Water is always being moved around in a cycle. Water evaporates from the land and sea and turns into water vapor. The water vapor is turned into clouds. The water in clouds then returns to the land as rain, snow, or hail. This water finds its way into rivers and streams and finally back to the sea.

This water cycle has been going on for millions of years. The rain you see falling today has fallen millions of times before.

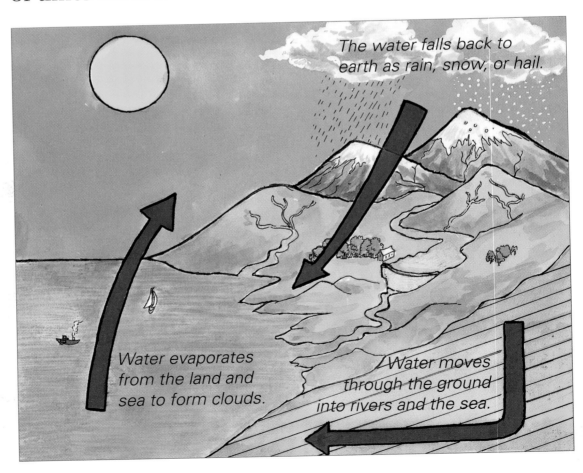

The water falls back to earth as rain, snow, or hail.

Water evaporates from the land and sea to form clouds.

Water moves through the ground into rivers and the sea.

WHAT MAKES IT RAIN?

The tiny water droplets inside clouds are constantly moving around. They bump into each other, join together, and slowly get bigger and bigger. When they get heavier, they start to fall, picking up smaller droplets on the way. Finally they fall out of the cloud as raindrops. We measure the amount of rain that has fallen using a rain gauge.

PROJECT

Make a rain gauge.

You will need
A clear plastic juice bottle
Scissors
A ruler
Some waterproof tape
A waterproof pen

1. Cut the top off the bottle. Get an adult to help you with the cutting.

2. With the ruler, draw a scale on the waterproof tape and stick it on the side of the bottle.

3. Fit the top of the bottle turned upside down into the base of the bottle.

4. Put the rain gauge in an open area in your backyard. (You may need to support it with some bricks to keep it from falling over.)

5. Record the rainfall once a day. If there is not enough rain to measure properly, you can write down "trace." Don't forget to empty the gauge after you have measured the rain each day.

SNOW

When it is very cold, the water droplets in clouds freeze into snow crystals. These crystals join together to make snowflakes. Snowflakes are always six-sided, and no two are ever alike. If the temperature remains below freezing while they fall, they will reach the ground as snow. Often, though, they will meet warmer air, melt, and turn into rain.

A coal train travels through a snowstorm.

The morning after a heavy snowfall .

HAIL

Hail only forms inside huge storm clouds. Tiny pieces of ice are blown around inside the cloud. They gradually get bigger as they collect more layers of ice on the way. When they get quite heavy, they fall out of the cloud as hailstones. If you ask an adult to cut a hailstone open, you will see the layers of ice that have built up inside it.

Hailstones in the grass.

RAINBOWS

Rainbows appear when it is raining and the Sun is shining at the same time. Sunlight is actually made up of six colors: red, orange, yellow, green, blue, and violet. When a ray of sunlight enters a raindrop, it is split up into all these colors, and these are what we see from the ground. You must have your back to the Sun to see a rainbow.

Rainbows actually form a complete circle. Because the Earth is in the way, you can only ever see half a circle from the ground.

Sometimes you can see the whole circular rainbow from an airplane.

An autumn rainbow.

DEW, MIST, FOG, AND FROST

Dew, mist, fog, and frost are also formed from water vapor in the air. Dew forms on cold, clear nights when water droplets condense onto cold surfaces such as grass, plants, or cobwebs. The dew evaporates when the Sun comes out during the day. If the temperature of the air falls below freezing, the dew turns to ice crystals and coats everything with frost.

▲ *Early morning dew on spider webs.*

Mist and fog are actually clouds that form near the ground. Like other clouds they are made when the air is full of water vapor. If the distance you can see is less than 0.6 mile (1 km), the cloud is called fog. Otherwise the air filled with moisture is called "mist."

It can be very dangerous driving in fog.

THUNDERSTORMS

Sometimes cumulus clouds grow into huge, tall cumulonimbus clouds. These clouds often bring thunderstorms. Static electricity that builds up in the clouds is released as a huge spark. This is what we see as lightning. The lightning heats the air as it passes, which expands very quickly and causes the crashing sound of thunder.

Because light travels faster than sound, you see the lightning before you hear the thunder. If you start counting when you see the lightning, you can work out how far away the storm is. For every 5 seconds you count, the storm is 1 mile (1.6 km) away. So if you count to 10, the storm is 2 miles (3.2 km) away.

HURRICANES

Sometimes when warm air rises over tropical oceans, it forms a very violent storm. In the United States and the Caribbean these storms are called hurricanes. They are also called typhoons, cyclones, or willy-willies in other parts of the world. Hurricanes bring very strong winds of up to 185 miles per hour (300 km/h).

Hurricanes rip up trees, destroy crops, and ruin buildings, sometimes flattening whole towns.

TORNADOES

The very worst storms of all are called tornadoes. Tornadoes are small, extremely powerful whirlwinds that form under thunderclouds. The wind speed inside them can reach 310 miles per hour (500 km/h). No one is sure how fast it is, since none of the instruments used to record wind speed has ever survived a really strong tornado! Tornadoes are most common in the Midwest where about 500 occur every year.

WEATHER FORECASTS

A prediction of the weather is called a weather forecast. To some people, weather forecasts are very important. Farmers need to know what the weather is doing, so they know the best times to sow, spray, and harvest their crops. Airports need to know when snow, fog, or ice are expected, so they can keep the runways open or close them. Fishers and other sailors rely on weather forecasts to tell them about the winds and weather they can expect at sea.

An impressive storm cloud builds up at the coast.

COLLECTING INFORMATION

In order to make weather forecasts, scientists called meteorologists collect information from all around the world. This information is sent in from thousands of weather stations on land, ships, and in aircraft. Weather satellites in space send down pictures of cloud formations.

All this information is fed into computers and studied by the meteorologists. Then they can make a picture of what is happening in the atmosphere and what weather can be expected in the next few days.

This satellite picture shows a hurricane developing off the coast of Mexico.

PROJECT

Be a weather recorder!

If you have carried out all the projects in this book, you will have enough equipment to make your own personal weather station. Using a small notebook, try recording the weather for a week.

Don't forget to measure:
- The amount of rain each day.
- The amount and type of cloud cover.
- The temperature at the same time each day.
- The speed and direction of the wind.
- The number of hours of sunshine each day.

CLIMATE

Climate is the pattern of weather a place receives over a long period of time. The climate of any area depends on its position on the Earth's surface. Lands near the equator have a hot climate because they receive more sunshine. Both the poles have very cold climates.

Climate also depends on how near the ocean a place is and how high it is. There are eight main types of climate.

A tropical rain forest in Costa Rica. Tropical rain forests grow in regions near the equator. They are warm all year round and have a high rainfall with rain falling nearly every day. Tropical rain forests are home to over half the animal and plant species in the world.

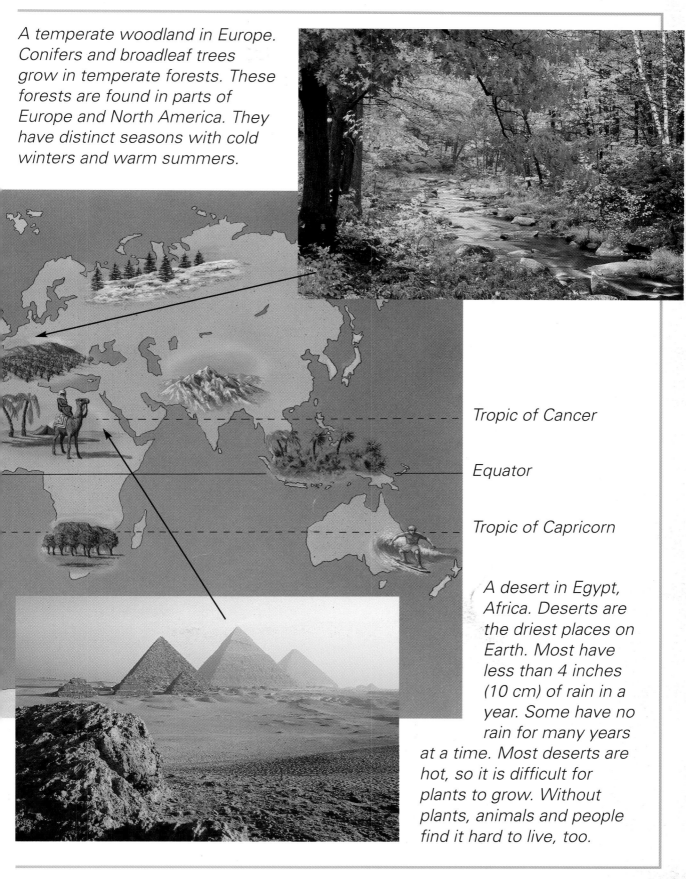

A temperate woodland in Europe. Conifers and broadleaf trees grow in temperate forests. These forests are found in parts of Europe and North America. They have distinct seasons with cold winters and warm summers.

Tropic of Cancer

Equator

Tropic of Capricorn

A desert in Egypt, Africa. Deserts are the driest places on Earth. Most have less than 4 inches (10 cm) of rain in a year. Some have no rain for many years at a time. Most deserts are hot, so it is difficult for plants to grow. Without plants, animals and people find it hard to live, too.

GLOSSARY

anemometer An instrument for measuring wind speed.

atmosphere The thin layer of gases surrounding Earth.

Beaufort Scale A scale of wind speeds.

climate The usual weather in a place, including temperature, wind, and rainfall.

condensation The process when water vapor cools and turns to water.

equator The imaginary line around the center of Earth.

evaporation The process when a liquid, like water, turns into a gas.

hurricane A very powerful, swirling storm.

meteorologist A scientist who studies the weather and the atmosphere.

season One of the four times during the year that has certain weather conditions.

temperature How hot or cold something is.

thermometer An instrument used to measure temperature.

FURTHER READING

Charman, Andrew. *Air.* (What About...? Series). Raintree Steck-Vaughn, 1994.

Davies, Kay, and Oldfield, Wendy. *Rain.* (See For Yourself series). Raintree Steck-Vaughn, 1995.

Farndon, John. *Weather: How to Watch and Understand the Weather and Its Changes.* (Eyewitness Explorers series). DK Publishers Inc., 1992.

Kerrod, Robin. *Weather.* (Learn about series). Marshall Cavendish, 1994.

Kramer, Stephen. *Tornado.* Lerner Publishers, 1992.

Llewellyn, Claire. *Wind and Rain.* (Why Do We Have? series). Barron, 1995.

Merk, Ann, and Meek, Jim. *Clouds.* (Weather Report Discovery Library). Rourke Corp., 1994.

The publishers would like to thank the following for permission to reproduce their pictures:

Bruce Coleman: Cover, Gunter Ziesler, page 5, top, 16, 17, (Dr Scott Nielsen), 21, top, (Andrew Purcell), 21, bottom, 23, top (Konrad Wothe); **Chris Fairclough**; page 26; **Gettyone Stone**: page 4, (Adamski Peek), 5, bottom, (Timothy Shonnard), 6, (David Olsen), 7, top, (Rob D. Casey), bottom, (Karl Weatherly), 10, (Donovan Reese), 12, (Patrick Cocklin), 14, (Mike McQueen), 14, (Paul Chesley), 20, (Don Spiro), 22, (David Woodfall), 23, bottom, (Jeremy Walker), 24, (Eddie Soloway), 25, top, (Cameron Davidson), bottom, (Alan R. Moller), 29, top (Larry Ulrich), bottom, (David Sutherland); **Oxford Scientific Films**; page 28 (Michael Fogden); **Science Photo Library**; page 27.

INDEX